ADEOTI ONAKOYA

IN GRIEF
I FOUND
GRACE

Foreword by

Pastor E. A. Adeboye
General Overseer, RCCG

authorHOUSE®

AuthorHouse™ UK
1663 Liberty Drive
Bloomington, IN 47403 USA
www.authorhouse.co.uk
Phone: UK TFN: 0800 0148641 (Toll Free inside the UK)
  UK Local: (02) 0369 56322 (+44 20 3695 6322 from outside the UK)

Published by AuthorHouse 12/14/2023

ISBN: 979-8-8230-8524-3 (sc)
ISBN: 979-8-8230-8525-0 (e)

Library of Congress Control Number: 2023919860

Print information available on the last page.

*Any people depicted in stock imagery provided by Getty Images are models,
and such images are being used for illustrative purposes only.
Certain stock imagery © Getty Images.*

*Cover Design by Motiff Design, Dublin
Layout: Motiff Design
motiffdesign@gmail.com*

*All scriptural quotations in this book are taken from the New King James
Version (NKJV), unless stated otherwise. In such cases they would be either
of the following: God's Word (GW), King James Version (KJV), New Living
Translation (NLT), or The Passion Translation (TPT).*

*Prosper's image courtesy of Cherry Orchard Photo Football Club
Cover image courtesy Depositphotos*

This book is printed on acid-free paper.

Contents:

Acknowledgements

Without certain people this book would not have been possible. These people played a prominent role in my life and my journey so far, especially during the trial and challenge.

First and foremost, all honour and adoration belongs to my ABBA FATHER; The Creator of life, who alone can change any story to bring Himself glory, and add value to life. Thank you LORD!

A mega appreciation to the General Overseer of The Redeemed Christian Church of God (RCCG) (Daddy G.O.); Pastor Enoch Adejare Adeboye, my father in the Lord, and to his wife, Pastor Mrs. Foluke Adeboye, my mother in the Lord. Thank you for the unbelievable privilege you gave my son Prosper and I. You sent your personal driver to bring us to your house for prayer. I will be forever grateful to you Sir and Ma.

My most grateful appreciation to all my spiritual fathers and mothers, most especially Pastor Adekunle Daniel, Provisional Pastor, RCCG Ireland and his wife, Pastor Mrs. Tokunbo Daniel. Thank you for your deep love, your words of encouragement, prayers, visitations, and always checking in on my family and I. God bless you Sir and Ma.

Thank you to the Regional Pastor of RCCG Ireland, Pastor Tunde Adebayo-Oke, and his wife Pastor Mrs. Caroline Adebayo-Oke. Thank you for your prayers and counselling during the tough and trying time. God bless you Sir and Ma.

With a heart filled with gratitude, I thank my family; RCCG Open Heavens Parish, both in Dublin and diaspora, for all your prayers during my trial. To the Pastors and Ministers in the house, all the youths, and young adults fellowship (20s on Fire!), thank you all so much. God bless you richly.

To my wonderful sister, Pastor Stella Toritsemotse and family. Thank you for your prayers and counselling. I truly appreciate all that you have done for me.

My beloved sister, Pastor Omoniyi Komolafe, for your prayers and encouragement to write this book; thank you! You were always looking forward to seeing this book.

To the Ogun Varsity Christian Alumni Fellowship (OVCAF) who organised the Overcoming Life's Challenges event at which I was a guest speaker, I say a huge thank you. Thank you for your prayers and encouraging me to put my story in a book to bless people's lives.

Thank you to Minister Janet Ajewole for being Prosper's favourite Aunty in church, and for your abiding advice during the tough period.

I am very grateful to Deaconess Roseline Akeredolu for standing by me spiritually as my prayer partner. Our prayers of intercession and agreement have gone a long way, especially in my emotional and mental healing.

A big thank you to Pastor Adunola Olugboun. The counselling I received from you brought much relief and helped me in becoming stronger. Thank you for the opportunity to speak at your programme in the area of bereavement.

I express my gratitude to Pastor Ayo Soyingbe. Thank you for your unconditional love for my family, your words of encouragement, and for ministering to us God's counsel.

Sister Ifesola Ifelaja, my adorable daughter, you are the angel that God sent to me when life got gloomy. I can never forget your words of comfort and assurance that played a part in my healing. I cannot stop thinking of your many words of comfort including: "Prosper is smiling at you right now". You texted me unexpectedly in the middle of the night and your words wiped the tears from my eyes. May the Everlasting Father remember you for good in Jesus mighty name. Amen.

Thank you to Pastor Obadare and all the Pastors at Hallelujah House, RCCG Camp, Ibadan, Nigeria, for all your prayers during our (Prosper and I) stay at Camp.

To my special Brother Elijah, the helper that God sent to transport Prosper and I throughout our stay at Camp. How could I have done all the moving around without your help? May the Almighty send you help Sir in Jesus name.

Thank you my Mummy Anifash at RCCG Camp, thank you Ma for all your love, care, empathy, and help during our stay at the RCCG Camp.

Thank you, my mother in the Lord in Nigeria, Evangelist Kikelomo Ali; the Founder of my beloved orphanage, Heritage Orphanage, Ibadan, Nigeria. Thank you for all your prayers, and letting me know that I can do all things through Christ who strengthens me. Thank you for checking in on my family and I all the time.

Thank you to Pastor Ademidun for his tremendous help during our time at RCCG Camp. Sir, you have been of great assistance to me.

A big thank you to Cherry Orchard Football Club, De La Salle Boys Primary School, St. Michael Primary School in Ballyfermot, including the Principals, teachers, pupils, and parents. You all contributed to making Prosper's academic experience a smooth and pleasant one.

My sincere gratitude towards my neighbours in Ballyfermot, including Mr. Sweeny, the former Commissioner of Peace at Ballyfermot, our beloved Independent Ballyfermot-Drimnagh Councillor- Sophie, and all the councillors at Ballyfermot.

My sincere appreciation goes to my entire family: The Adegboyega family and Onakoya family. Thank you for all your help that you displayed in one way or another.

With a grateful heart, I say a big thank you to my children who have always been a source of encouragement at every stage of our journey.

To my great editor and co-writer, my daughter Peace Onakoya. Without you, this book would not have been completed. Thank you for all the late nights with me, encouraging me to start this book. You were always available even when I got tired of writing. You did not allow me to stop. May my ABBA FATHER send a Helper of Destiny to you in the time of your need in Jesus mighty name. Amen.

To my darling husband who has stood by me, and affirmed me. You have loved me beyond anything that I could have imagined at the start. Thank you for being the man that I needed to help me at every season. You have been my pillar and support even when I doubted myself. You really believe in me, and even, beyond my expectations. I am very thankful for your prayers and love for me and our family. Your daily prayers for me, I believe, is one of the reasons why I am strong today. You always remind me that my success, hope, blessing, joy, and treasure can only be found in the hands of The Living God. Many times, I forget that you are going through the same emotions as I am. You always make your shoulder available for me to lean on. You are my number one fan, always celebrating my effort no matter how little it is. I am grateful to The LORD for you, my husband.

The list of acknowledgements is unending, for space I honestly cannot mention everyone but my God will thank you all for me and reward you in a mighty way. You will not cry over anything that gives you joy in Jesus' mighty name. Amen

Huge thank you to everyone for your love!

Foreword

Grace is the sure anchor whenever the ship of life is tossed up and down the troublesome waters. It is one special gift that God bestows on His children, especially in grieving moments.

The chilly nature of losing a love-one could frozen the heart of anyone without the grace of God.

Adeoti Onakoya has not only chronicled this saddest and poisonous experience of life, but has poignantly demonstrated, through her personal experience, how the grace of our Lord Jesus Christ and His words of life can pilot a man successfully through this storm of life, without being overwhelmed.

Everyone has one lesson or the other to learn in this articulately dramatised diary.

I recommend it without any restraint.

Pastor E. A. Adeboye
General Overseer, RCCG

Preface

I would like to thank God for the grace and courage He gave me to pass through the journey of my trial. It was a long walk. A long walk. I did not even realise how far I had come until I began to put pen to paper. And as the ink stained the paper to form a new sentence, I took another step down the long distressing road. I thought that I would have someone write the story on my behalf but it turns out that no one could really navigate the path of this journey apart from me.

I would often ask the question: "why me? Why did this have to happen to me?" It was perplexing to me as I have not sown evil seeds to reap such a harvest *(Galatians 6:7)*. However, John 16:33 implies that no one is above tribulation. I learned to trust God's Word which says "all things work together for good to those who love God" *(Romans 8:28)*. Do not misquote this verse, it is either good or bad things that can happen, but God gives His children the assurance that everything will work together for their good. Praise God, Hallelujah! So we count it all joy when tribulation happens *(James 1:2-4)*.

It is this assurance in Christ Jesus that I want to share with anyone who may or will go through challenging times, and this is my reason for writing this book. As you read this book, you will be at a greater advantage than I was when I was dealing with the challenging times. You now have insight to all the wisdom I learned; what worked well, and what did not on the journey. All this knowledge is derived from the Bible. The Bible is the source of God's Word on earth which contains His knowledge and wisdom. This is the ultimate authority for the Christian, proving to be unfailingly true always, in and out of space and time.

I chose this topic: **"In Grief, I Found Grace"** because I personally discovered the grace of God that is upon my life during a trying time of my life. This was in finding strength to move on, discovering and developing my passion, and becoming an author. I would have never thought that I could be a writer. It is solely by the grace of God, Hallelujah. I do not know how I would be still standing here today, if not by the God's grace. Truly "in grief, I found grace".

Dedication

I have the joy in my heart to dedicate this book to my hero and my son, **Late Prosper David Oluwateniola Onakoya**. Out of sight, is not out of mind. Thank you for striving to fulfil your promise to me since you were younger. It was because of you, I flew for the first time in my life with first class on-board British Airways. In the last hour of your life, you brought it to pass!

You will forever remain in the centre of my heart, my love. Thank you for being strong until the end. I continually feel the palm of your hand rubbing against mine, as you did at RCCG Camp. Anytime I would cry, you were there to console me.

Rest In Peace, My Love.

And to everyone who has overcome trials and challenges with God's grace, and for those that are still battling with life, or are still going through one thing or another, I celebrate and applaud you all!

CHAPTER ONE
The Story Of My Trial

"My brethren, count it all joy when you fall into various trials, [3] knowing that the testing of your faith produces patience. [4] But let patience have its perfect work, that you may be perfect and complete, lacking nothing."

- James 1:2-4

Sunday, 7th February 2016

I woke up and realised that he was not breathing.

My son had stopped breathing right beside me. I yelled for the cabin crew to help. They tried cardiopulmonary resuscitation (CPR) again and again, but it was to no avail. Then, a doctor pronounced him dead. 'My son died in my presence', I thought. 'How could I not have noticed?' I held him tight to my bosom and poured water on his body. 'It's not true, it's not true. He mustn't be dead.' But he was long gone. His body had started becoming cold. I put my ear to his chest, but there was nothing to hear. Endless droplets flooded down my face. Sorrow had swallowed me up, I was overcome with emotion. Unaware of what was occurring around me, I just stared. 'Was I still on the plane coming back from Nigeria, or was I dreaming?' What a nightmare! I pinched myself, but I was not asleep. This was no nightmare. I wished it was. It was the saddest day of my entire life. I'd rather be the one dead. This experience was so weighty, my head went numb and my heart froze cold. It felt like my breath was ceasing. 'Am I dying too?'

"Adeoti, do you have any other children"

"It doesn't matter", I cried. "Leave me alone"

I could not think of anyone else. At that moment, it seemed like my only son had died and his body laid lifeless before my very eyes. 'How would I break this news to his father and his siblings?'

I thought back to how God had blessed me with them. People doubted that I could give birth to children. "She can never have children. She doesn't have a womb. I pity her husband…" Imagine having people say things like this at your own wedding. My wedding day came on the 16th January 1999, and these were the words of gossip uttered at the venue. Even with these poisonous comments, it was still a glorious day. Every time I look back, I am filled with gratitude that I did not have to wait long to get married, nor was there any delay in childbearing.

Although he was dead, I could see the prayer of my father coming to fulfilment. On my wedding day he prayed "As the mountains surround Jerusalem, so shall your children surround your table"; and that is exactly what happened. As the years went by, God blessed my husband and I with seven children; four girls and three boys. The fourth and fifth children were both boys. They were like twins; having less than a year's difference in their ages. They looked alike, and shared interests alike. Those interests ranged from preaching to sports.

When Prosper, the fourth child was a toddler, he acted like a pastor. He only wore suits, and was always with a small bottle of anointing oil, a mini microphone, and a Bible. His favourite preachers were Bishop Ayo Oritsejafor from Delta State, Nigeria and Pastor Ade Okonrende from Houston, Texas, but especially Pastor Ade Okonrende. He had a keen interest in Prosper, and anticipated seeing him every time he came to Ireland. Every opportunity Prosper had to watch or listen to Pastor Oritsejafor and Okonrende, he would do so earnestly like his life depended on it; and what he listened to and watched was exactly what he became. He would stand on the table, hold his microphone to his mouth, and preach. He preached and preached and preached, and as he preached, it seemed like his words were no longer that of a child messing around, but divinely inspired. Profit, the fifth child, was known as his assistant pastor. They were like partners in ministry. Seeing my sons like this put a smile on my face and warmed my heart with joy because it was clear that they were on the right path.

As they grew up, so did their love for football as well. Many football clubs desired to sign them up onto their team. They played for the best clubs in the Dublin District Schoolboys League (DDSL) and the League of Ireland. Prosper was the captain of his team; Cherry Orchard football club. He was often titled 'Man-of-the-Match'. He was nicknamed 'Yaya Touré' after the famous African midfield football player, but his favourite football player and role model was Cristiano Ronaldo from Portugal. Prosper and his brother represented their club around the world, in countries such Holland and England. My husband and I even had the opportunity of visiting Manchester and Liverpool stadium because of them. They never ceased to make us proud.

Then, one chilly October's night in 2015, Prosper began to vomit vigorously. It was the worst we had seen him. His face was pale and he progressively became feeble. His coach would later testify of a change in his performance in football. When my husband and I took him to see the General Practitioner (GP), he was prescribed a certain medication. However, it failed and his health began deteriorating drastically. At this point, we were startled and troubled as it was unusual for such to occur in our family. Before then, we rarely had a cause to take our children to the hospital for ill health-related issues. The perfect health the Lord had blessed the family with was always common and evident among us all.

However, this situation was atypical, therefore we were compelled to revisit the hospital. On this occasion several tests were conducted. Our hearts pounded as we anxiously anticipated to receive the results. 'What exactly could be wrong..? What is taking them so long..? Nothing bad must happen to my son in Jesus name...' my husband and I thought as we waited in uncertainty. And what we were told was not what we ever expected to hear:

"After conducting various tests... We checked his blood pressure, tested his urine.... But we still weren't sure as to what exactly was going on..."

"What do you mean you're not sure? We have been waiting here for a long time."

"We apologise about the delay, but I need you to remain calm please. Please."

"How can we remain calm? It's our son we are talking about here."

"Okay, okay. So our final resort was to scan his brain. And what we found was-

"Yes, yes, what is it? What did you discover?" we impatiently interrupted, anxious about our son's wellbeing.

"We discovered an aggressive brain tumour in the left side of his brain."

"What? It cannot be true. I reject it in the name of Jesus. It's not our portion in Jesus name" we replied, rebuking the diagnosis.

Before I knew it we were transferred to another hospital and shown the image of his brain with the tumour in it. It was brought to our knowledge that the tumour could not be removed. It had grown quite large and deep underneath his skull. The doctors said that there was no medical cure and the only probable remedy was radiation therapy. The treatment was designed to target the cancer cells, but it would simultaneously damage his brain's function. Therefore, as they said "he would not live long", but his life would be preserved for just a few more years.

> *'Why me?*
>
> *Why did this happen?*
>
> *How could this have happened?*
>
> *Where is God?'*

Questions. These became like a familiar friend constantly revisiting my mind every day. I was often lost in my thoughts. There was no sense to be made out of the current events. Not knowing the cause or any favourable natural solution, we sought God's divine help and intervention. We all embarked on continuous prayer and fasting. My family, my church, my Pastor and his wife. Day and night, night and day, we prayed, and prayed, and prayed...

A couple of days passed and we were contacted to commence the treatment. I gazed at my son in dejection. *'If I let him undergo the treatment, I would lose my smart, active, and intelligent boy. He would become a vegetable...But he could be around for a bit longer. If I forbid him from undergoing the treatment, he may die sooner...Or, God would miraculously heal him?'*

I thought to myself. I kept going back and forth weighing my options. It felt like the worst ever decision, and my husband and I were forced to give our verdict. I had to measure the risk and the probabilities of the given possibilities. This was about to be the toughest decision we had ever made.

We finally decided to take him to the Redeemed Christian Church of God (RCCG) Camp, Lagos, Nigeria in December 2015 instead. Our goal was for him to be prayed for by Pastor Enoch Adejare Adeboye (the General Overseer). By this time, Prosper was approaching the climax of his illness after just 2 months since the terrific vomiting experience. He could barely walk, was extremely frail and feeble, suffering from short-term memory loss. Unfortunately, Prosper and I were not able to meet Pastor E.A. Adeboye, but we prayed in our hearts that God will harken to us and heal our son at the altar in the main Auditorium of RCCG Camp.

As we continued seeking Prosper's healing, it felt as though we were going around in circles. From one recommended place to another. Still, we never gave up. We later took him to another hospital in the UK to look for better options or solutions. We took him there but the diagnosis was the same, and the only medical solution was radiation therapy.

At this point all hope seemed lost, and so many negative thoughts filled my mind. I saw myself drowning in the sea of depression. I had fallen into a place that got darker and darker by the day. I completely forgot about my wellbeing and that of my other children. My entire focus was fixed, working on the recovery of Prosper; but he got worse day by day.

He went from being strong to weak, he could no longer uphold his own body mass. From walking to being lame, from remembering to forgetting, and from seeing to even losing his own eyesight. He could barely eat and rarely used the toilet. Everything seemed like it was going from bad to worse but still, I never gave up.

My spirit kept nudging me to take Prosper back to RCCG camp. I had witnessed how God has used Pastor E.A. Adeboye to heal many people with cases worse than Prosper's, even to raise people from the dead. It was so convincing that I could not resist it. So in late January 2016 we returned to RCCG camp. Fortunately, we had the opportunity to meet Pastor E.A. Adeboye this time. He had just returned back from his travels and he requested to see us privately. Prior to seeing him, we had written a letter in advance to him describing the situation and attaching supporting documents to it. Thankfully, we were in camp when he requested for us, sending his own personal driver to pick us up.

Meeting Daddy Enoch Adejare Adeboye was such an uplifting experience that gave us so much hope. He prayed for Prosper and encouraged us. I was sure from that point that my son was healed. It was so evident in his immediate miraculous recovery. Prosper, who was unable to use the toilet for 10 days, excreted that very same day. His swollen face and eyes had gone back to normal. The joy that filled my heart was beyond words. Hope was inevitable. I would not have to bury my son, he was beginning to heal.

We stayed a few more days in Camp before returning home. Throughout the time we spent in Camp; before and after we met Pastor Adeboye, we had so many reasons to thank God. There were numerous encounters from God, Him sending favour and help to us, particularly in places such as the Hallelujah House in RCCG Camp. I certainly cannot tell it all.

On our way back from Nigeria, we were upgraded from economy to first class due to Prosper's condition. It was our first time flying first class. Prosper had begun to fulfil the promises he made to me. How he would take me around the globe in first class, buy me a golden house and car, and so on. The memory of these promises brought tears to my heart.

I looked at my son lying next to me, 'would he be able to fulfil all of them? Only God knows', I thought and I cried myself to sleep that night.

Then suddenly, I woke up and realised that he was not breathing anymore...

CHAPTER TWO
My Response

"And He said to me, "Son of man, can these bones live?""

- Ezekiel 37:3

As living beings one of the characteristics that God has blessed us with is the ability to respond to stimuli; the changes in our environment. These changes range from migrating to a new country or school, getting married, and even the death of a loved one is no different.

The ability to respond to stimuli only lies within the living and for this reason it is checked by the paramedic before conducting Cardiopulmonary Resuscitation (CPR). It is so crucial, as response is the beginning of adaptation, and adaptation is essential for living.

So what was my response to the death of my son?

1: Feelings & Emotions

"A fool expresses all his emotions, but a wise person controls them"
- Proverbs 29:11 (GW)

The Bible tells us that the human being is composed of a spirit, has a soul, and lives in a body.

"Now may the God of peace Himself sanctify you completely; and may your whole spirit, soul, and body be preserved blameless at the coming of our Lord Jesus Christ." - 1Thessalonians 5:23

Each one of us are spirits, we have a soul, and we live in a body. The real person reading these words is a spirit. And in us is our primary source of knowledge concerning our life. The scriptures say:

"For what man knows the things of a man except the spirit of the man which is in him? Even so no one knows the things of God except the Spirit of God." - 1 Corinthians 2:11

Originally, God intended for this primary source of knowledge to be His word in our spirits. And today, this should be so for the born again child of God, as that was what brought about their new birth.

"[18] Of His own will He brought us forth by the word of truth... [21]... receive with meekness the implanted word..." - James 1:18-21

Our soul consists of our consciousness, sub-consciousness, and imagination. Our consciousness includes our will, emotions, feelings, and intellect. These are the parts of our soul that we are aware are at work right now. In contrast, the subconscious is the programmable part of our soul that runs our life in the background without our awareness, for example, when we are asleep.

The spirit, soul, and body are all interconnected. The spirit connects to the soul through our imagination. That is intangible hearing, sight, and perception. The spirit and soul both share this ability. The soul is in touch with the body through its will. The body then connects back to the soul through its five senses which it also uses to interact with the natural world. When there is a stimulus in our environment, one or more of five senses discerns it, and the body communicates it to the soul.

Oftentimes, the first method of reaction the soul employs is our emotions. We may become excited, downcast, or enraged. For example, *"Jesus wept"* at Lazarus' grave in *John 11:35. Job 2:13* says that Job's *"grief was very great"*. And David expressed joy and happiness in *2 Samuel 6:14-17* when he *"danced before the Lord with all his might;"* The soul is supposed to receive knowledge on what to do, especially in response to stimuli, from the spirit that will inform its will. The problem is that, ever since the fall of man in Genesis chapter 3, spiritual death has substituted the source of knowledge of the natural man for his five senses instead of the Word of God.

"[3] But of the fruit of the tree which is in the midst of the garden, God has said, 'You shall not eat it, nor shall you touch it, lest you die.' [6] …the woman…she also gave [the fruit] to her husband with her, and he ate. [7] Then the eyes of both of them were opened, and they knew that they were naked;… [11] And He [God] said, "Who told you that you were naked? Have you eaten from the tree of which I commanded you that you should not eat?" - Genesis 3:3, 6-7, 11

So because the spirit of the fallen man is dead, the soul has no source of knowledge in the Word of God anymore. It just lets the data picked up by the senses inform its will and responds based on how it feels. Therefore, humans naturally live based on what they feel and think, leading to carnality. The problem with feelings is that they can be as unstable as water; constantly fluctuating from time to time, therefore living based on them is like building a house on sinking sand.

While feelings are valid, God did not create them for us to solely live by. They are not supposed to dictate and determine the course of our lives. Only the Word of God can do that. One of the reasons God has given us our emotions is so that we can sympathise and empathise with one another. This helps us, as people, to connect with each other, and to relate with those around us on an intimate and personal level.

While grieving Prosper's death I experienced a rollercoaster of emotions. Some moments I'd be sorrowful, then other times angry, then calm, or regretful. Each stage before and after his death brought about a new set of emotions to live with. When he fell sick, and died, there was an immense weight of shock that gripped my heart. There was an abounding presence of despair when searching for answers. Although, when I encountered people who had gone through worse, I felt a little relief of gratitude.

During my trial, one thing that I learned was to never make decisions based on how I feel, but rather the truth. In contrast with one's feelings, the truth is void of assumptions. I learnt the harder way to choose the truth of God's Word over my feelings. It was not easy, but I can most certainly say that when I did this, it set me free as Jesus said that it would in John 8:32:

"And you shall know the truth, and the truth shall make you free." - *John 8:32*

It caused me to trust God over what I thought. And my God, that was a lighter burden to bear *(Matthew 11:28-30)*!

While our feelings are valid, we must not allow them to occupy the place of the truth of God's word, and prevent us from acting upon it.

2: The Pain of Grief

"Jesus wept" - John 11:35

I cannot deny, the pain of Prosper's death still remains present with me till today. From the day the doctor gave us his report, to his death, and even now as I write, it has all been a painful experience; an experience filled with pain.

Although, bringing my pain and grief to God made a huge difference. Counsellors, therapists, and doctors can try to numb the pain, but only God, the Great Physician can heal the wounds of the soul with His Word.

The Bible says: *"For the word of God is living and powerful, and sharper than any two-edged sword, <u>piercing even to the division of soul and spirit,</u> and of joints and marrow, and is a discerner of the thoughts and intents of the heart."* - Hebrews 4:12

God's word has the capacity to reach the unreachable parts of our heart and soul and mend the broken pieces. My advice therefore is to:

1. Bring your problems to Jesus.

Jesus beckons, appeals, and implores us to do so in Matthew 11:28 and 1 Peter 5:7.

"Come to Me, all you who labour and are heavy laden, and I will   give you rest." - Matthew 11:28

"...casting all your care upon Him, for He cares for you." - 1 Peter 5:7

You should not wallow in frustration and pain, because He said "bring them to Me". Through your hardship, find comfort in God's Word.

"For whatever things were written before were written for our learning, that we through the patience and comfort of the Scriptures might have hope." - Romans 15:4

And remember that God's Word is "yes and amen", meaning it is certain *(2 Corinthians 1:20).*

The Word of God is not just facts and statistics that are subject to change, but it is the truth that is constant forever. Therefore, you can wholeheartedly rely on it.

2. Focus on Jesus, the Word of God, rather than the size of your problem.

Just like Joshua with the wall of Jericho, God promised them victory when He asked them to go around the wall seven times. Joshua did not doubt the word of God, He trusted God's word and did exactly what God had instructed, and the walls came tumbling down *(Joshua 6:2-4, Joshua 6:20-21; Hebrews 11:30).*

"[2] And the Lord said to Joshua: "See! I have given Jericho into your hand, its king, and the mighty men of valor. [3] You shall march around the city, all you men of war; you shall go all around the city once. This you shall do for six days… [4] But the seventh day you shall march around the city seven times, and the priests shall blow the trumpets. " - Joshua 6:2-3

"[11] By faith the walls of Jericho fell down after they were encircled for seven days." - Hebrews 11:30

Similarly, you must trust in God's plan even when it seems not to make sense. No matter how big your problem may seem, be rest assured that you will come out of it triumphantly!

In the Book of Job, we see a "blameless and upright [man], one that feared God, and shunned evil" *(Job 1:1)*. Job suffered the pain and agony of loss. He had lost his children, all his possessions, and his perfect health.

[15]…when the Sabeans raided them and took them away—indeed they have killed the servants with the edge of the sword; and I alone have escaped to tell you [Job]!"

[16] While he was still speaking, another also came and said, "The fire of God fell from heaven and burned up the sheep and the servants, and consumed them; and I alone have escaped to tell you!"

[17] While he was still speaking, another also came and said, "The Chaldeans formed three bands, raided the camels and took them away, yes, and killed the servants with the edge of the sword; and I alone have escaped to tell you!"

[18] While he was still speaking, another also came and said, "Your sons and daughters were eating and drinking wine in their oldest brother's house,

[19] and suddenly a great wind came from across the wilderness and struck the four corners of the house, and it fell on the young people, and they are dead; and I alone have escaped to tell you!" - Job 1:15-19

[7] So Satan went out from the presence of the Lord, and struck Job with painful boils from the sole of his foot to the crown of his head. [8] And he took for himself a potsherd with which to scrape himself while he sat in the midst of the ashes. - Job 2:7-8

His situation was so unfortunate that his wife advised him to "curse God, and die" in Job 2:9 in order to escape the situation. Oftentimes, people frown upon this woman for giving such counsel, and say that she was supposed to comfort Job. But how can the suffering comfort the suffering, unless divinely helped by God? Likewise, not only I, but my entire family suffered from the pain of the loss of Prosper. When facing a challenge or a trial, be aware that those around you may also be affected by it as well. They may not shed tears or talk about it, still, that should not subject their concealed feelings to invalidity.

3:   Bargaining & Bitterness

"The Lord is near to those who have a broken heart, And saves such as have a contrite spirit." - Psalm 34:18

As human beings, grieving the loss of a precious possession can be unbearable. We may believe that we cannot live without that thing or person, that we need them to survive, or that they were not meant to come to an end. This may then lead us to negotiating for an extension of its existence with other powers, or reflect on how we could have prevented its extinction:

> *"If only I had done this, or that to help him to recover..."*
>
> *"I shouldn't have done this, I should have done that..."*
>
> *"God, if you heal/restore them, I will..."*

This is known as bargaining and can be a part of the grieving process. It was a bad habit that I had to part with. Bargaining can cause bitterness, resentment, and regret, especially when our negotiations go unfulfilled.

For me, I could not find answers to the cause of Prosper's sudden illness and death; it was so unexplainable, and I began to blame myself for the death of my son:

"Was I not fervent enough in prayer? I should have taken my children for check-ups more regularly... Should I have allowed him to eat food from others? Lord God, please heal my son and I will never do that again..."

I held a grudge against myself for a while and struggled to forgive myself for what I did or did not do.

For others, they may blame God, begin to question His existence and power, or even try to earn His goodness by making vows and promises. While inquisitively asking God questions to understand and get to know Him is permissible, questioning His person must be avoided. This is because questioning God has two dimensions that differ by motive. The first is questioning God to learn more about His person and His thoughts. The second is questioning God from a place of resentment towards Him, doubting the existence of His person, and undermining His authority. God is all-knowing; He sees exactly what you are going through, and most importantly, He cares and can feel the pain!

"[14] Seeing then that we have a great High Priest who has passed through the heavens, Jesus the Son of God, let us hold fast our confession. [15] For we do not have a High Priest who cannot sympathise with our weaknesses, but was in all points tempted as we are, yet without sin." - Hebrews 4:14-15

Instead of questioning God from a place of resentment and doubt, let us learn from Job and our Lord Jesus Christ in the Bible. These people both went through tough times. Job was stripped of almost everything he had in a day. Our Lord Jesus Christ was nailed to the cross for sins that He did not commit. Instead of doubting God, resenting Him, or undermining His power, Job confronts God to ask Him questions about His predicament.

"[20] "Have I sinned? What have I done to You, O watcher of men? Why have You set me as your target, So that I am a burden to myself? [21] Why then do You not pardon my transgression, And take away my iniquity? For now I will lie down in the dust, And You will seek me diligently, But I will no longer be." - Job 7:20-21

Although there may be some ignorance in his speech, we can see that he still believes in God and does not in any way doubt God's existence and authority. Likewise, our Lord Jesus questioned God similarly while on the cross.

"And about the ninth hour Jesus cried out with a loud voice, saying, "Eli, Eli, lama sabachthani?" that is, "My God, My God, why have You forsaken Me?" - Matthew 27:46*

In both scenarios, we see that their questions sought God's heart, will, and mind concerning their state. But in doing this, they did not resent God, doubt His existence, or undermine His power in their life. Also, because Jesus never sinned (according to *2 Corinthians 5:21* that says: "... He… [Jesus] who knew no sin…"), we know that it is not a sin to ask God questions. In fact, our Heavenly Father loves when His children come boldly to His throne of grace especially in tough times, to seek His heart, help, will, and fulfil it.

"Let us therefore come boldly to the throne of grace, that we may obtain mercy and find grace to help in time of need". - Hebrews 4:16*

For this reason, David is called "a man after God's heart" in *Acts 13:22.* He sought the heart of God by pondering on His Word and being inquisitive. Think about it, how else will we learn more from God's heart if we do not ask Him questions?

Bargaining is pointless and only leads to a deadly end. Instead of negotiating and investigating what you did right or wrong, learn to forgive yourself and others. Realise that you have already done what you have done or what you knew to do best. Do not harbour unforgiveness in your heart. It can prevent you from going far in life by keeping you stuck in the past.

"bearing with one another, and forgiving one another, if anyone has a complaint against another; even as Christ forgave you, so you also must do." - Colossians 3:13*

Therefore, forgive yourself, and stop blaming yourself for the situation.

Know that in the good and bad God is a good God. He not only sees all that you are going through, but He cares and can sympathise with you (Hebrews 4:15). So do not try to earn His goodness. He is good and does what pleases Him, that is, that which is good. And He will bring good from the bad loss.

"For the Lord is good; His mercy is everlasting, And His truth endures to all generations." - Psalm 100:5

"But our God is in heaven; He does whatever He pleases." - Psalm 115:3

4:   Rejection, Loneliness & Isolation

"When my father and mother forsake me, Then the Lord will take care of me." - Psalm 27:10

When you experience an unusual loss that many people cannot identify with, you can feel lonely. When you are discriminated against or treated as an outcast, you can feel rejected. And when you are separated from the crowd by yourself or others, you can feel isolated.

There were days I felt lonely. Lonely. Though people were around, I still felt lonely. Then lonely again when I was actually on my own. It would be logical to think that being in the midst of such a great company would be consoling, but that is not always the case. Having comforters around you is very helpful, but what about when your comforters have no experience of what you are passing through? This loneliness is more psychological, where those around can only feel sorry for you, but cannot feel what you are going through as well.

"Stop crying!" "Life must continue!" The pain of hearing that cliché and being forced to face the reality of it was frightening. "Life must continue without my son", I thought. Eventually, the days came when I was literally on my own. My comforters and their counsel had slowly faded away. Gradually, everybody started moving on, visits from friends and family decreased. Phone calls and messages ceased. They had to resume their daily activities.

I would be taken aback by the way I was treated and related to. It was as if people had so quickly forgotten that I had witnessed the beginning and end of my very own son's life. I was looked down upon and hurt from different sides, even by relatives. They may forget that you are still grieving and are so quickly agitated, frowning at your unintended irrational actions, if any, because they simply just do not understand the pain you are going through. This caused me to feel rejected. I became angry, thinking, "why did this have to happen to me?"

When it feels like you are all alone and there is not one person that can relate to you, know that there is One who says "I will never leave you, nor forsake you" (Joshua 1:5). His name is Jesus! You may think that people do not care about you, but that is not always the case. Human comforters are limited in capacity and come with their frailties, there is only so much that they can bear and do. Only Jesus will be with you six weeks, six months, six years from the loss, and even forever.

If you are familiar with loneliness, you will agree that it is addictive in a way, you may like the silence, and enjoy being alone. I would often be engulfed in my lonely state. Staring at the ceiling in darkness, lost in my thoughts. I did not want to be in the company of people, and when I was, I said very little. You should know that as human beings, we were not created to function this way. Our Creator said in Genesis 2:18 that "It is not good for man to be alone..." Connect with people, be part of a lively, supportive Church, and communities, attend different events, meet new people. It takes a lot of effort at first and you may still feel sore and lonely, but overtime the cloud of isolation will be lifted, and the weight of loneliness will soon dissipate.

5: Disappointment

"Now hope does not disappoint, because the love of God has been poured out in our hearts by the Holy Spirit who was given to us." - Romans 5:5

"But that's not what's supposed to happen!" We often hear these words when there's a plot twist in a story, when the food does not turn out according to the recipe, or when scientists do not get the results that they anticipated in an experiment. Sometimes we have expectations, but what happens in physical reality can be contrary to them. Then, we become disappointed. Disappointment is the natural way to feel when our expectations are not met, when a dream/desire becomes unfulfilled, or when that which we hoped for is not what we get. It goes without saying that as long as we have expectations, disappointment is a possibility.

"Hope deferred makes the heart sick, But when the desire comes, it is a tree of life." - Proverbs 13:12

From the beginning to the end of my trial, the journey was filled with numerous moments of disappointments. From the day that we got Prosper's diagnosis, until he took his final breath, things just did not turn out to be the way I thought they should. My children have just always been healthy from birth, no complications whatsoever to the glory of God. If someone had predicted Prosper's death beforehand, I would with all confidence and faith in God denied it. I certainly did not foresee his illness, and even at that, I hopefully awaited his total recovery. However, that's not what happened. So if there is anyone who knows what it means to be disappointed, it is me!

Someone may ask: "if disappointment can only occur when one has expectations, why not get rid of all expectations?" Firstly, we must realise that disappointments are the product of unfulfilled expectations, and not expectations in general. These expectations are formed and influenced by our experiences, laws, and principles. Secondly, we see in Galatians 6:7-10, the word of God implies to us to expect the reward/outcome of whatever it is we sow.

"[7] Do not be deceived, God is not mocked; for whatever a man sows, that he will also reap. [8] For he who sows to his flesh will of the flesh reap corruption, but he who sows to the Spirit will of the Spirit reap everlasting life. [9] And let us not grow weary while doing good, for in due season we shall reap if we do not lose heart. [10] Therefore, as we have opportunity, let us do good to all, especially to those who are of the household of faith."
- Galatians 6:7-10

In fact, the Word urges us to start planting good seeds in faith based upon this truth. What is faith? According to *Hebrews 11:1* "... faith is the substance of things hoped for, the evidence of things not seen." It is by it we; children of God, are supposed to live.

"For in it [the Gospel of Jesus Christ] the righteousness of God is revealed from faith to faith; as it is written, "The just shall live by faith. - Romans 1:17

God expects us to live believing His Word, and expecting its fulfilment in our lives; its physical manifestation because being expectant is an evidence of faith. Therefore, to get rid of all expectations would not be biblical. (To learn more about faith see part 9. Faith & Fear in this chapter.)

In order to avoid unnecessary disappointment, I would advise the following:

1.   Have expectations according to the Will of God.

One can know if their expectations are according to the Will of God, when the Word of God supports them.

"By faith we understand that the worlds were framed by the word of God, so that the things which are seen were not made of things which are visible." - Hebrews 11:3

Let the Word of God be the source of all your expectations because by the Word do the physical realities we expect come into existence. We should make our expectations according to the Word of God because…

I.   God is interested in bringing about the fulfilment of His will.

"Your kingdom come. Your will be done On earth as it is in heaven." - Matthew 6:10

When our expectations are according to His Word, they are according to His will, and then, they can be sponsored by His Spirit; the Spirit that creates life and realities as seen in *Genesis 1:2.*

"But if the Spirit of Him who raised Jesus from the dead dwells in you, He who raised Christ from the dead will also give life to your mortal bodies through His Spirit who dwells in you." - Romans 8:11

II. He, being the beginning and the End as He said in Revelations 1:8 knows everything to come and that was. Therefore, nothing catches Him by surprise, He can never be disappointed. We can therefore trust Him and His Word.

2.   Commit your expectations to God in prayer.

"Be anxious for nothing, but in everything by prayer and supplication, with thanksgiving, let your requests be made known to God;" - Philippians 4:6

Prayer allows us to...

I.   Commit our desires to God, and appeal for His help.

  "Trust in the Lord with all your heart, And lean not on your own understanding; In all your ways acknowledge Him, And He shall direct your paths." - Proverbs 3:5-6

II.   Prayer allows us to see ourselves receiving the physical manifestation of our requests. The Word of God, in *Mark 11:23,* encourages us that when we ask for something in prayer, the key to receiving it is to believe that one has it.

  "Therefore I say to you, whatever things you ask <u>when you pray, believe</u> that you receive them, <u>and you will have them</u>." - Mark 11:24

III.   One cannot believe without expecting. Do not just mention your desires/requests to God, <u>you must see it</u>! Bring them to life through meditation using the eyes of your soul to see them. Your soul connects to your spirit through your imagination. In your spirit God has imparted are all the possibilities and promises of God that are in the spirit realm.

  "Blessed be the God and Father of our Lord Jesus Christ, who has blessed us with <u>every</u> spiritual blessing in the heavenly places in Christ," - Ephesians 1:3

  In your spirit is where the Spirit of Jesus; who is the fullness of God resides (Colossians 2:9).

You must transport them from the spiritual realm to the physical using your imagination, words, and actions:

"For as he thinks [imagines] in his heart, so is he. "Eat and drink!" he says to you, but his heart is not with you." - Proverbs 23:7

"Death and life are in the power of the tongue [words], And those who love it will eat its fruit." - Proverbs 18:21

"For as the body without the spirit is dead, so faith without works [actions] is dead also." - James 2:26

When the Spirit of God sees you doing this (demonstrating faith), He imputes His power to bring the imagination/expectation to life. Your thoughts and words can communicate with God!

IV. In prayer, we can also get guidance from the Holy Spirit (John 16:13) on how to go about our expectations and doing the following steps:

3.   Applying the principles of the Kingdom of God in faith to bring your expectations to manifestations. For example, the law of seed-time and harvest is one of the principles of the Kingdom of God as seen in *Galatians 6:7-10*:

"[7] Do not be deceived, God is not mocked; for whatever a man sows, that he will also reap. [8] For he who sows to his flesh will of the flesh reap corruption, but he who sows to the Spirit will of the Spirit reap everlasting life. [9] And let us not grow weary while doing good, for in due season we shall reap if we do not lose heart. [10] Therefore, as we have opportunity, let us do good to all, especially to those who are of the household of faith." - Galatians 6:7-10

This law has never failed us. Even unbelieving farmers apply it and get results. You must search the scriptures to find all the principles of the Kingdom. All the principles that we need to succeed in this life, God has hidden in it. It is not enough to expect/have faith, you must take steps *(James 2:17-19, 26).*

[17] Thus also faith by itself, if it does not have works, is dead. [18] But someone will say, "You have faith, and I have works." [19] Show me your faith without your works, and I will show you my faith by my works.   - James 2:17-18

For example, a woman who wants children and a blessed family, should not expect a virgin birth like Mary because the Word of God says "...be fruitful and multiply..." *(Genesis 1:28).* After doing the first two steps, she must do the needful. Applying the laws of the kingdom is proof that you actually have faith in the Word of God, and are therefore acting upon it.

Review your expectations, dreams, or goals, and ensure that they are in-line with the Word, the Will, and principles of God. Isaiah 55:8, 11 says:

"[8] For My thoughts are not your thoughts, Nor are your ways My ways," says the Lord. [11] So shall My word be that goes forth from My mouth; It shall not return to Me void, But it shall accomplish what I please, And it shall prosper in the thing for which I sent it." - Isaiah 55:8,11

God does not think the way humans normally think so we must confirm that our expectations are aligned with how He thinks as revealed in His Word. Only the Word of God guarantees fulfilment.

When learning to do the steps that have been outlined, it is possible to make mistakes, which can of course lead to disappointments. ***So if disappointed, do the following:***

1.   Know and understand that God can still use our disappointments for His appointed purpose in our lives. God the Holy Spirit works endlessly to ensure that our lives are going in the direction and will of God for us.

"[26] Likewise the Spirit also helps in our weaknesses. For we do not know what we should pray for as we ought, but the Spirit Himself makes intercession for us with groanings which cannot be uttered. [27] Now He who searches the hearts knows what the mind of the Spirit is, because He makes intercession for the saints according to the will of God. [28] And we know that all things work together for good to those who love God, to those who are the called according to His purpose." - Romans 8:26-28

Our compliance just makes the task simpler. The occurrences in our lives, no matter how big or small are of massive concern to Him, He looks deeply into their details.

2.   Talk to the Holy Spirit, a spiritual leader, mentor, pastor, or a **christian friend that you trust** about your situation so they can lead you to the right direction.

"Where there is no counsel, the people fall; But in the multitude of counsellors there is safety. - Proverbs 11:14

Try not to keep the disappointment, let it out, have it dealt with so your faith does not waver because of it.

3.   Keep up the faith.

"I have fought the good fight, I have finished the race, I have kept the faith." - 2 Timothy 4:7

6: Regret

"Then Judas, His betrayer, seeing that He had been condemned, was remorseful and brought back the thirty pieces of silver to the chief priests and elders, saying, "I have sinned by betraying innocent blood." And they said, "What is that to us? You see to it!" Then he threw down the pieces of silver in the temple and departed, and went and hanged himself."

- Matthew 27:3-5

Disappointment and regret can often go hand-in-hand. What happens when you expect something based on a principle/law/ideology that you believe in, then make a decision based on it, but the contrary happens? You may regret that decision, especially if its effects are dreadful.

The most painful thing about having regrets is that we cannot naturally go back to undo the events, we do not have a time machine, and we may not be able to forget about it. We may think we have forgotten about it but a little stimulus comes, and it feels like it only happened yesterday.

Looking back, there are so many things that I wish I could change, do, or undo, that I think would have prevented Prosper's illness and death. Is it taking him to better healthcare, is it permitting the therapy as well as taking him to Nigeria for prayers, or is it keeping his condition private?

For example, after Pastor E.A. Adeboye had prayed for my son, I saw massive improvements in his health. Suddenly, he could use the toilet after not doing so for 10 days. He seemed to have gained strength in his body. It was like he was coming alive again. A fountain of joy began to spring from within me. My hope was coming to life and my expectations were closely within reach. I could see the light they promised was at the end of the tunnel. Although, that's not how the story ended. I was advised by a family member to bathe Prosper with a certain herbal treatment. After which, his health seemed to deteriorate again. At the time, I did not see any harm in it. I did not realise that using such was essentially putting my faith in something other than God. Could it have been the hindrance to his successful recovery?

As the saying goes, "if only I knew". But you would not have known, that is the point! We have to realise that at that time our decisions may have been the best decisions we knew to make and we made the decision based on the information available. I would have never, on purpose, used something on my son knowing fully well that it would cause his death. And you would not have taken that step if you knew it would have negative implications.

Use the past as a compass to make better decisions, there is no other way to deal with regrets than to receive God's mercy and forgiveness, learn from it, and move on.

"When Jesus had raised Himself up and saw no one but the woman, He said to her, "Woman, where are those accusers of yours? Has no one condemned you?" She said, "No one, Lord." And Jesus said to her, "Neither do I condemn you; go and sin no more."" - John 8:10-11

Once you have received salvation and the forgiveness of sins that has been made available through the death of Jesus Christ, there is no need to beat yourself up about that mistake or sin. It no longer exists because God has righteously wiped it away *(Romans 3:25-26)*. Hallelujah!

"Therefore, if anyone is in Christ, he is a new creation; old things have passed away; behold, all things have become new." - 1 Corinthians 5:17

(To learn more about the gift of salvation and how to receive it, see chapter 5 of this book).

Trust God that He will convert what caused harm for our good because He is a good God. He knows how to go about accidents, mistakes and regrets.

If you have it in mind or feel like hurting yourself or committing suicide, please and please talk to someone you trust, fast. Talk to God, receive the forgiveness that He has made available for you, and forgive yourself. There is no sin that is too big for God to forgive because of the more-than-sufficient sacrifice of Jesus Christ. Suicide is _not_ the way out!

7: Vulnerability

"[9] And He said to me, "My grace is sufficient for you, for My strength is made perfect in weakness." Therefore most gladly I will rather boast in my infirmities, that the power of Christ may rest upon me. [10] Therefore I take pleasure in infirmities, in reproaches, in needs, in persecutions, in distresses, for Christ's sake. For when I am weak, then I am strong."
- 2 Corinthians 12:9-10

Going through emotional turmoil can render one to be weak and vulnerable. The creation of a soft-spot in one's soul. It may expose one to the possibility of threat and harm physically, spiritually, or physiologically. Throughout the journey, I found myself in and out of this state.

When I was in transit in London, the airline I flew with, British Airways, took me to an office for a brief counselling session before allowing me to return back to Ireland. Prosper's body was taken away from me. It was taken to the mortuary and an autopsy was conducted on it. The British Airline manager accompanied me, but I felt all alone. I could sense a void inside of me like a precious part of me had been stripped away from me.

Then I had to continue the journey; taking the next connecting flight to Dublin on my own. The experience of Prosper's death flashed before me and the tears came surging in again, blurring my eyesight. With a swollen face and a lump in my throat, I took my seat alone. The manager turned to me and said "take it easy, you will be fine, your son is gone, there is nothing that you can do about it", in an attempt to console me. A couple of minutes passed, then she brought me a photo of a man with a long beard and said, "If only you will believe in this man, he will give you peace." I looked at the picture, and he was clearly not Jesus Christ, Prince of Peace *(Isaiah 9:6)*. If it were a figurative picture of Jesus, I would not have minded, but it was not. It was another god. "Jesus is the way, the truth, and the life *(John 14:6)*. There is no other god elsewhere", I hollered...

As life went on, I found that more people attempted to take advantage of my vulnerability. Many people tried to bully me, control me, and manipulate me. Some would deal harshly with me, while others would offer harmful advice and lies that are contrary to the Word of God. I became confused and felt like I was being experimented with. Different suggestions and ideologies were presented to me from the left, right, and centre.

Whilst it is true that God can minister to us through people, we must also be aware of false prophets and teachers; counsel that appears right but is utterly evil and deadly. We must keep from every appearance of evil *(1 Thessalonians 5:22)*.

"[1] Beloved, do not believe every spirit (we learned in 1. Feelings/Emotions that humans are spirits), but test the spirits, whether they are of God; because many false prophets have gone out into the world. [2] By this you know the Spirit of God: Every spirit that confesses that Jesus Christ has come in the flesh is of God, [3] and every spirit that does not confess that Jesus Christ has come in the flesh is not of God. And this is the spirit of the Antichrist, which you have heard was coming, and is now already in the world." - 1 John 4:1-3

The life of Job demonstrates the importance of this admonition. After he had lost everything, his council of friends circled him. They began to provide their hypotheses, theories, and philosophies concerning his matter. Though there was some degree of truth in some of their words, it could not fully provide an answer to Job's problem. And we see God rebuke them in *Job 42:7-17*.

"[7] And so it was, after the Lord had spoken these words to Job, that the Lord said to Eliphaz the Temanite, "My wrath is aroused against you and your two friends, for you have not spoken of Me what is right, as My servant Job has. [8] Now therefore, take for yourselves seven bulls and seven rams, go to My servant Job, and offer up for yourselves a burnt offering; and My servant Job shall pray for you. For I will accept him, lest I deal with you according to your folly; because you have not spoken of Me what is right, as My servant Job has." - Job 42:7-8

When one is vulnerable, especially when they are grieving, people often suggest their ideas concerning the grieving's situation, their opinions and thoughts. There will also be false teachers and counsel presented.

Oftentimes, they are not obvious to sight. Satan is conniving and subtle. He can even use close family to achieve his aim. This is how he executed his plot on Adam in the Garden of Eden. Satan was aware that Adam was fully aware of the commandment of God not to eat the fruit of the Garden of Eden. He also knew that the only way for him to get to Adam was by going through Eve as Adam had a soft-spot for his wife Eve. He cunningly used this to bring Adam's downfall. Adam found it difficult to resist eating the fruit that she offered him because he loved her. This is what led to him sinning against God *(Genesis 3:1-7).*

When Vulnerable endeavour to do the following:

1.   Become acquainted with the Word of God.

"[21] Now acquaint yourself with Him [the Almighty God], and be at peace; Thereby good will come to you. [22] Receive, please, instruction from His mouth, And lay up His words in your heart.

Becoming acquainted with the Word of God is becoming acquainted with God because just as you cannot separate a person from their words, you cannot separate God from His Word."

"[1] In the beginning was the Word, and the <u>Word was with God</u>, and <u>the Word was God</u>. [14] And the <u>Word became flesh and dwelt among us</u>, and we beheld His glory, the glory as of the only begotten of the Father, full of grace and truth." - John 1:1,14

Therefore God is His Word, and His Word is God. This Word became a person in human form and He was given the name Yeshua; that is Jesus.

"And she will bring forth a Son, and you shall call His name Jesus, for He will save His people from their sins." - Matthew 1:21

We can therefore have fellowship, intimacy, and a relationship with the Word of God. This is vital for every single moment of the believer's life, especially when vulnerable. The Word of God is food (Matthew 4:4), and it will provide one with strength to not be subject to ungodly counsel. The Word of God is a sword and the helmet of salvation that the Christian is commanded to put on *(Ephesians 6:17)*.

Knowing the Word of God intimately will help us to identify, decipher and reject ungodly counsel.

2.   Pray with the Holy Spirit (this means talking to God with the language of the Holy Spirit (*1 Corinthians 14:2*). It is God's divine language that He gives every Christian to speak at will when He comes upon them as seen in *Acts 2:1-17*).

"But you, beloved, <u>building yourselves</u> up on your most holy faith, <u>praying in the Holy Spirit</u>," - Jude 20

This scripture tells us that this is how we build ourselves with the faith of God as our foundational structure. Strong faith is essential as the enemy will try to attack the Word of God on the inside of us as described in the Parable of the Sower (Matthew 13:1-3, 5, 20-21) when we are weak/vulnerable. He will give a million and one reasons to deny God and His existence. We must remember that he is a liar and the father of liars (John 8:44)! If God were not real, why is the devil so concerned as to whether we believe in Him or not? Our faith is like infrastructure, it can be built, attacked, and demolished. It is also our shield that we can use "to quench fiery darts of the enemy", such as ungodly counsel (Ephesians 6:16). How strong is your faith?

3.   Know; *have the knowledge, and believe* with the entirety of your heart ***that God is your Defender.*** When we are weak, He is our strength (2 Corinthians 12:9). He shields us with His wings like the mother-hen does her chicks.

"He who dwells in the secret place of the Most High shall abide under the shadow of the Almighty." - Psalm 91:1

Therefore, know that you are protected and loved.

4.   Surround yourself with other believers committed to the same goal; with the same focus. Look for people who are in right-standing with God to pray with. By the grace of God, He will turn your mess to a message, your story to glory in Jesus' mighty name. Endeavour to keep good companions who will affect you positively.

"He who walks with wise men will be wise, But the companion of fools will be destroyed." - Proverbs 13:20

But beware, not every friend is fit for every chapter in the book of your life.

5.   Show vulnerable people, including yourself, mercy. Anyone without the mercy of God is as good as dead.

"Through the Lord's mercies we are not consumed, Because His compassions fail not." - Lamentations 3:22

We must show mercy to one another. Do not neglect or run from people during their challenges or trials. Show the love of God, care and concern for them. Have a good word of encouragement that imparts grace to them and aligns with the word of God (Ephesians 4:29). If you do not show mercy to others, you cannot see the mercies of God.

"Blessed are the merciful, For they shall obtain mercy." - Matthew 5:7

Jesus shows us what this looks like in Matthew 18:21-35.

8: Faith & Fear

"I am crucified with Christ: nevertheless I live; yet not I, but Christ liveth in me: and the life which I now live in the flesh I live by the faith of the Son of God, who loved me, and gave himself for me." - Galatians 2:20

"There is no fear in love; but perfect love casteth out fear: because fear hath torment. He that feareth is not made perfect in love." - 1 John 4:18

Faith and Fear are opposites of each other. The Kingdom of Light operates by faith, but the Kingdom of Darkness by fear. While walking in faith means adopting and accepting the Word of God as the truth and only believing it. Fear on the other hand, is the same but with the lies of the devil and this physical world. It is the opposite of the God-kind of faith. Throughout the journey, there was a constant battle between these two in my mind.

When Prosper was extremely sick, there were many recommendations and suggestions coming from each and every direction. The doctors' reports would only testify that my son's state was deteriorating. Different people gave all sorts of advice on how to handle the plight. They would recommend foods and juices to give him, and places to take him. While others would help to investigate and deliberate the cause of his sickness and death. My own thoughts would wander and search out the different possibilities and outcomes available. All these were numerous voices speaking to me that greatly influenced my mind-set, sometimes causing my level of faith to fluctuate. And fear would rise up. My faith was being tested. I had to consciously and purposefully try to focus on God's Word to remain faith-full; full of faith.

We must be careful what we expose our eyes and ears to. What we hear and see can affect what we believe because our convictions, values, and in turn, our actions stem from them. As humans, we follow our persuasions more than anything else. The ideologies in our subconscious minds programme and run our lives.

"Keep your heart with all diligence, For out of it spring the issues of life." - Proverbs 4:23

Our lives are reflections of what we truly believe.

Faith is the Word of God that substantiates desires and things hoped for and is evidence of the things that cannot be seen.

"Now faith is the substance of things hoped for, the evidence of things not seen." - Hebrews 11:1

The Word of God is the ultimate, trusted, and authorised evidence of the things that do exist in the seen and unseen world because by the Word were all things created *(John 1:3).*

Faith is the only authorised way to come to God to receive anything from Him according to *Hebrews 11:6* and *Mark 11:22-24.* It is the bridge that transports the spiritual realities that are found in God's Word into this physical world. This is because it is the language of love that appropriates what the loving God *(1 John 4:7)* has already made available for us through the sacrifice of Jesus Christ.

"For in Christ Jesus neither circumcision nor uncircumcision avails anything, but faith working through love." - Galatians 5:6

Real, living faith of God always results in a confession, then an action that is in-line with the Word of God that is believed.

"[18] But someone will say, "You have faith, and I have works." Show me your faith without your works, and I will show you my faith by my works. [19] You believe that there is one God. You do well. Even the demons believe—and tremble! [20] But do you want to know, O foolish man, that faith without works is dead? [26] For as the body without the spirit is dead, so faith without works is dead also." - James 2:18-20

"...God, who gives life to the dead and calls those things which do not exist as though they did;" - Romans 4:17

All the Patriarchs in the hall of faith of Hebrews 11, believed something about God and His Word, this caused them to do something or say something in-line with it.

Abraham believed that God had a plan for him when He told him to leave his father's house *(Genesis 12:1-3)*. He believed that he was the father of many nations and responded positively to that name when God called him that *(Genesis 17:5)*. He also believed that God would provide a sacrifice when he went up to offer Isaac *(Genesis 22:8)*.

"[20] He [Abraham] did not waver at the promise of God through unbelief, but was strengthened in faith, giving glory to God, [21] and being fully convinced that what He had promised He was also able to perform." - Romans 4:20-21

Noah built an Ark before seeing any sign of floods because He believed in God's word *(Hebrews 11:7; Genesis 6:13-22)*.

"By faith Noah, being divinely warned of things not yet seen, moved with godly fear, prepared an ark for the saving of his household, by which he con-

demned the world and became heir of the righteousness which is according to faith." - Hebrews 11:7

David stood up to fight Goliath because he believed that "the battle is the Lord's." (1 Samuel 17:45-47). These people not only believed God with a mere mental assent but they were persuaded by what they believed and acted accordingly. Their actions stemmed from their believing and their persuasion in the Word of God. God calls this living righteously.

"...The just shall live by faith." - Romans 1:17

"[21] and being fully convinced that what He [God] had promised He was also able to perform. [22] And therefore "it was accounted to him for righteousness." - Romans 4:21-22

And today, we read in awe of the mighty results that were produced in their lives as seen in Hebrews 11:32-38.

Anyone who is born of God; who has the Holy Spirit living inside them has this God-kind of faith.

"...the life which I now live in the flesh I live by the faith of the Son of God, who loved me, and gave himself for me." - Galatians 2:20 (KJV)

And they have the command to always operate by it (Romans 1:17). The problem is that they may not always do so.

How to operate by faith:

1. Fellowship with the Word of God purposely and continuously.

"So then faith comes by hearing, and hearing by the word of God." Romans 10:17

The Word for "hearing" in this verse means "to give audience" to the Word in the original translation. There are many ways to do so. For example, by reading, listening, studying, and especially meditating on the Word.

2. Pray, especially in the Holy Spirit (Jude 20).

3. Speak like God.

"We having the same spirit of faith, according as it is written, I believed, and therefore have I spoken; we also believe, and therefore speak;" - *2 Corinthians 4:13*

As a child of God, your words have the same creative power of your Father. You can speak what you want to be according to His Word and expect it to occur *(John 15:7).*

4. Act like God's word is true, because it is true.

"Sanctify them by Your truth. Your word is truth." - John 17:17

However, it is important that as we take positive steps in response to God's living Word that we remain led by the Holy Spirit when doing so. Never be ahead or behind Him *(Romans 8:14).*

9: Waiting on God in the Place of Prayer

"But those that wait upon the Lord Shall renew their strength; they shall mount up with wings like eagles, They shall run and not be weary, They shall walk and not faint." - Isaiah 40:31

Prayer is a communicative form of fellowshipping with God. When we pray to fellowship with God, we become transformed into the image of the One we are praying to.

"As He [Jesus] prayed, the appearance of His face was altered, and His robe became white and glistening." - Luke 9:29

This transformation includes an impartation or transference of many spiritual possibilities that are in God. This includes an impartation of God's kind of strength.

Throughout the tough times there were constant periods of waiting. Waiting. For the next hospital appointment, for God's healing power to touch my son, waiting to arrive at the next prayer meeting, and waiting to be healed from the wounds of loss. I waited a lot. These seasons were the 'make or break' periods of my faith. I would either meditate on the lies that Satan would fire into my imagination. Or, the Word of God and God's acts of love in the past. I found that there is nothing like waiting in the place of prayer.

The Bible says in *Psalm 46:10* says *"Be still, and know that I am God"*. In order for us to know God intimately, there is a need for stillness and waiting that are essential. We know God by fellowshipping with Him.

When we do this, the Holy Spirit is given the liberty to do His Ministry (see Chapter 3: The Ministry of the Holy Spirit and His Word).

"But those who wait on the Lord Shall renew their strength; They shall mount up with wings like eagles, They shall run and not be weary, They shall walk and not faint." Isaiah 40:31

This passage of scripture says that when we wait on God, our strength is renewed so that we can fly, run, and walk without getting tired. The word for "wait" here is "qâvâh" in Hebrew. It means to bind or intertwine together. It speaks of bonding with the Lord. Just as the strength of a rope increases the more strings are intertwined to make it, even so we rise in strength when we bond in fellowship with the Lord. When we bond with the Holy Spirit, He takes us from one level to another in glory (2 Corinthians 3:18). The Word of God instructs us not to stop engaging in this activity of waiting in the place of prayer.

"pray without ceasing," - 1 Thessalonians 5:17

Today, I can say that I am a living testimony of the Spirit of God's healing and strength from this place of prayer.

When waiting on God, be immersed in spiritual practices of value. These includes:

1. Prayer (and fasting).

"[1] Then Jesus, being filled with the Holy Spirit, returned from the Jordan and was led by the Spirit into the wilderness, [2] being tempted for forty days by the devil. And in those days He ate nothing, and afterward, when they had ended, He was hungry. [14] Then Jesus returned in the power of the Spirit to Galilee, and news of Him went out through all the surrounding region." - Luke 4:1-2, 14

Jesus' 'potential power' (fullness of the Holy Spirit) was converted to 'kinetic power' (power of the Spirit) as He waited on the Lord in prayer added with fasting. Ironically, when we fast and pray, we actually increase in true strength, capacity, and power, which are spiritual.

2. **Engaging with the Word of God**, especially by listening to it, meditating on it, and speaking it out loud. *(Joshua 1:8; Proverbs 6:20-23)*.

"[20] My son, keep thy father's commandment, and forsake not the law of thy mother: [21] Bind them continually upon thine heart, and tie them about thy neck. [22] When thou goest, it shall lead thee; when thou sleepest, it shall keep thee; and when thou awakest, it shall talk with thee. [23] For the commandment is a lamp; and the law is light; and reproofs of instruction are the way of life:" - Proverbs 6:20-233.

3. **Be thankful to God.**

"in everything give thanks; for this is the will of God in Christ Jesus for you." - 1 Thessalonians 5:18

Remember that not because of everything, but in everything, we ought to give thanks to God. By doing so we will not quench, but encourage the ministry of the Great Comforter; the Holy Spirit in us *(1 Thessalonians 5:19)*.

4. **Be engaged in the work of God.**

10: Continuing In The Work Of God

"...My grace is sufficient for you and my strength is made perfect in your
weakness" - 2 Corinthians 12:9

When the Apostle Paul felt a "thorn in the flesh" *(2 Corinthians 12:7)*,
he felt weak. He sought to the Lord more than once for the pain to leave
him, but it did not. Then the Lord spoke His word of encouragement
that brought him grace and strength. The same word which is our above
quote. Eventually, Paul began to see from the Lord's perspective and explained that our weakness allows for the power of God to work more
effectively. Not that God causes pain and hardship, but He can turn it
around for His glory.

"So now I am glad to boast about my weaknesses, so that the power of
Christ can work through me." - 2 Corinthians 12:9 (NLT)

I often would find myself distressed like Paul at various times during the
trial. For example, on my initial trip from Nigeria, I was on the plane
heading to Dubai to get a connecting flight to Ireland. I had not got-
ten the opportunity to meet with Pastor E.A. Adeboye. My heart was
heavy, my expectations were cut short, and my eyes were swollen from
the tears I cried looking at Propser's worsening condition. I decided to
spend some time reading my Bible to be encouraged by the Word of God.
As I did, there was a man who sat next to me, he was on his way to the
United States. He inspected me curiously as I read and asked, "are you
a Christian?" I replied "yes", welcoming the window of opportunity to
evangelise. We spoke for most of the journey, our words tickling the ears
of other passengers. Just like many in the world, he believed that there is

a god, but he was not a Christian and did not see the need for church. He had been suffering from the hurt of back-stabbing friends and so-called Christians who had duped him. The Holy Spirit enabled me to preach the Good News to him and he listened calmly and attentively to my words like they were that of a higher authority. With amazement he asked how to understand the Bible. My simple answer was "the Holy Spirit". I told him about my spiritual parents Pastor and Pastor Mrs. Okonrede and the church they pastor in Houston Texas. And from that day on salvation came to him and his household.

One cannot minister to change the belief system of an individual naturally. It requires the engracing of the power of God. This power is most effective when we are weak because when a person is weak, it means that they lack power and have little or no strength or ability of their own to perform a given task. The power of God works more effectively in this state because it is not in competition with any other power including our human ability. It can flow and manifest exclusively because we begin to depend on the Lord totally for strength and grace. And thus this is one of the reasons for fasting. Fasting rids our flesh of its natural source of power that sponsors its daily activity- food. As a result, the Christian relies totally on the power of God that is supplied to her (Apostle Paul and I can attest to that!).

Our weakness attracts God because…

1. God loves us and is compassionate towards us.

2. It allows for the Kingdom of God that is in power to come (1 Corinthians 4:20).

   Where the power of God is at work, His influence can dominate, and where His influence dominates, His rule is established, and where His rule is established, His reign and Kingdom has come. And subsequently, His will is done *(Matthew 6:10)*.

What is this will? The same Apostle Paul said to Timothy that it is for *"all men to be saved, and to come unto the knowledge of the truth" (1 Timothy 2:4)*.

One of the things I have learned throughout this journey is that no matter what one is passing through, you must not let it stop you from doing the Work of God, preaching the Gospel of Christ, and impacting lives. This is because in your weakness, the power of God is most effective. Even in the midst of trials, pain, and hurt, it is still possible to be a blessing. You may be thinking; "but Mrs. Adeoti, how is that possible?" By the Spirit of God! In *1 Corinthians 2:1-5*, Apostle Paul describes his experience when he went initially to present the Gospel to the Corinthians. He says *"I was with you in weakness, and in fear, and in much trembling."* Despite that, he was still able to win souls to the Kingdom because his words were "in demonstration of the Spirit and of power". *"It is not by power nor by might"* of man, the Lord says that it is *"by my Spirit".* Many believers, including pastors, have things that they are all going through. Nevertheless, we can still be a blessing to our generation because we host the Spirit of God, and therefore the presence of God. It was not our competence that qualified us to be used by God, and therefore our incompetence cannot disqualify us. The Lord can do as He pleases through us because His Spirit and power has come upon us making us His portals into this world. Your qualification and competence to do the work of God is the Spirit of God upon you. Glory be to God!

It should not be misinterpreted that things like good character, skills, and academic qualifications are not useful when it comes to ministry. They are, in fact, really useful. However, they cannot qualify us for the work of God. They cannot supersede the power of the Holy Spirit in doing the work of God.

Therefore, so long as you remain connected with God, you will have access to the power for doing His work.

"Then He [Jesus] <u>appointed</u> twelve, that they might <u>be with Him</u> and that He might <u>send them out to preach</u>," - Mark 3:14

Thus, our appointment in the Kingdom of God is dual in nature: 1) to be with Jesus (it is from our relationship with the Lord that we access His power *(Matthew 28:18-20)*. And only then, 2) to preach (and there are many ways to do this).

CHAPTER THREE

The Ministry of the Holy Spirit and His Word

"But the Comforter, which is the Holy Ghost, whom the Father will send in my name, he shall teach you all things, and bring all things to your remembrance, whatsoever I have said unto you." - John 14:26 (KJV)

When navigating the course of this life, there are two things that are essential for direction: 1) The Spirit of God and 2) The Word of God. These are the two resources that God has given us of Himself. The Word of God is our map. It shows us the journey of life from God's perspective; through God's eyes, God's desires for us, and the roads to take to get there. The Holy Spirit is like our modern day Global Positioning System (GPS). He shows us how to use the map to get to our destination, prescribing the exact steps and directions to take. The Word sets distinct and firm bounded roads, and the Holy Spirit helps us navigate the path outlined. The Holy Spirit is the author of the Word of God.

"... [20] knowing this first, that no prophecy of Scripture is of any private interpretation, [21] for prophecy never came by the will of man, but holy men of God spoke as they were moved by the Holy Spirit." - 2 Peter 1:20-21

Without the Holy Spirit, we are bound to wrongly interpret the Word of God.

"[10] But God has revealed them to us through His Spirit. For the Spirit searches all things, yes, the deep things of God. [11] For what man knows the things of a man except the spirit of the man which is in him? Even so no one knows the things of God except the Spirit of God. [12] Now we have received, not the spirit of the world, but the Spirit who is from God, that we might know the things that have been freely given to us by God." - 1 Corinthians 2:6-16

This is dangerous because the Word of God is a sword (Ephesians 6:17). Using it wrongly can lead to severe damage, even death, instead of life.

"as also in all his epistles, speaking in them of these things, in which are some things hard to understand, which untaught and unstable people twist to their own destruction, as they do also the rest of the Scriptures." - 2 Peter 3:16

Only the owner of the sword; the Holy Spirit, knows how to properly use and engage it. Therefore, as believers, we need both the Spirit and the Word. If one focuses on just the Word, one could become too religious. And religiosity kills a vibrant relationship with God, and exposure to the supernatural. If one focuses just on spiritual things without the Word, they could get lost in the spiritual realm unable to decipher and discern the leading of God from the leading of the devil. The Spirit and His Word work hand-in-hand. The Word cannot work without the Spirit, and the Spirit won't work without the Word. We see them co-labouring during the creation of the world in the beginning *(Genesis 1:2-3; John 1:1-3).*

The Word of God and the Spirit of God were essential in my recovering and healing from the loss of my son- Prosper. They both showed me the path of escape to take and how to take it in the journey of my trial, even to where I am today.

"No temptation has overtaken you except such as is common to man; but God is faithful, who will not allow you to be tempted beyond what you are able, but with the temptation will also make the way of escape, that you may be able to bear it". - 1 Corinthians 10:13

They provided me with many lessons, experiences, and encounters that brought comfort and edification.

Part 1
The Holy Spirit My Comforter

*"Blessed be God, even the Father of our Lord Jesus
Christ, the Father of mercies, and the God of all comfort;
Who comforteth us in all our tribulation, that we may
be able to comfort them which are in any trouble, by the
comfort wherewith we ourselves are comforted of God."*
- 2 Corinthians 1:3-4

The Holy Spirit is not fire, He is not wind, He is not oil, and He is not a cloud. He is not even a dove. Although, He can appear or seem like these forms, He is a person; an individual personality:

1.   He has a mind.

"Now He who searches the hearts knows what the <u>mind of the Spirit</u> is, because He makes intercession for the saints according to the will of God."
- Romans 8:27

2.   He has a will.

"But one and the same Spirit works all these things, distributing to each one individually <u>as He wills</u>." *- 1 Corinthians 12:11*

3.   He can speak.

"Then <u>the Spirit said</u> to Philip, "Go near and overtake this chariot."" *- Acts 8:29*

4.   He can hear.

"However, when He, the Spirit of truth, has come, He will guide you into all

truth; for He will not speak on His own authority, but _whatever He hears He will speak;_ and He will tell you things to come." - *John 16:13*

5. He has feelings.

"And do not grieve the Holy Spirit of God, by whom you were sealed for the day of redemption." - Ephesians 4:30

6. He can move.

"The earth was without form, and void; and darkness was on the face of the deep. And the Spirit of God was hovering over the face of the waters." - Genesis 1:2

7. He can interact/fellowship.

"The grace of the Lord Jesus Christ, and the love of God, and the communion of the Holy Spirit be with you all. Amen." - 2 Corinthians 13:14

The Holy Spirit a person of the Trinity. Therefore, He is equally God as the Son (the Word) is and the Father is also.

"For there are three that bear witness in heaven: the Father, the Word, and the Holy Spirit; and these three are one." - 1 John 5:7

He is the Spirit of God *(Genesis 1:2)*. He has always been instrumental and active in bringing to manifest the will of the Father, especially in these end times. After Jesus left the earth, the Father sent the Holy Spirit to be with us, in us *(John 14:17)*, and upon His children *(Acts 2:3-4, 17, 33)*. His assignment for this generation (both Christians and non-Christians) is listed in *(John 16:7-14)*. To the believer, He is the 'Allos Parakletos' [Greek]; Helper; Comforter; Counsellor; Intercessor; Standby; and Advocate.

"[16] And I will pray the Father, and He will give you <u>another Helper</u> [Allos Parakletos], that He may abide with you forever— [17] <u>the Spirit of truth</u>, whom the world cannot receive, because it neither sees Him nor knows Him; but you know Him, for He dwells with you and will be in you. [26] But the <u>Helper, the Holy Spirit,</u> whom the Father will send in My name, He will teach you all things, and bring to your remembrance all things that I said to you." - John 14:16-17, 26

The Holy Spirit is my Allos Parakletos, meaning He is just like Jesus but a different kind. Pastor Benny Hinn calls Him "Jesus unlimited", speaking of His presence. And through the journey of my life He has consistently been this, my companion, and more. No one else could have brought me out of the darkest moments when I felt like the day could never break again. I saw His hand in I) teaching and reminding me of the Word of God, II) comforting, strengthening, and edifying me, and in III) manipulating the desires and emotions within me.

I

The Ministry of the Holy Spirit in Teaching me and Reminding me of the Word of God:

The Holy Spirit is extremely passionate about the Word of God. His major goal is the exaltation of the Word; who is Christ. He is attracted to where and any opportunity that this can be done. He does this by revelation.

"He will glorify Me, for He will take of what is Mine and declare it to you." - John 16:14

The Holy Spirit is the Spirit of Revelation, this is when He manifests as both the Spirit of Knowledge and Understanding simultaneously. As Jesus said in John 16:14, He takes the data of the Word ("He will take of what is mine"), brings it to the believer ("and declare it to you"), and then gives the understanding too (John 14:26). This is how the children of God can hear from God. The Holy Spirit has the ability to act upon the Word of God like enzymes do to food, and break it down by imputing the understanding the more we chew, on the Word. There were two major instances when this phenomenon occurred during my recovery from the loss of my son.

The first time, I had a dream one fateful night. I dreamt I saw my son Prosper saying to me "Mummy, I ran out of the grave." This was my first revelation after his death.

The second was when I stumbled upon a Bible verse while I was having my morning devotion. I did not plan to come across this verse but the Lord directed me to it.

"And God will wipe away every tear from their eyes; there shall be no more death, nor sorrow, nor crying. There shall be no more pain, for the former things have passed away." - Revelation 21:4

Throughout my Christian life, I had never encountered this verse before. Yes, I would have heard it at church services and other Christian events, or maybe I had even read it before. Nonetheless, I had never had a personal encounter with this Word until then. The Holy Spirit had quickened the revelation of this verse to me in that instant.

It is the spirit that quickeneth [gives life]; the flesh profiteth nothing: the words that I speak unto you, they are spirit, and they are life. - John 6:63

This verse of scripture was spoken by Jesus Christ of Nazareth. It means that it is the spirit of a person that gives life to their body. The Holy Spirit gives life to the Logos of God (the knowledge of God) and makes it the Rhema of God (revelation-knowledge of God). This is the Word of God, that when spoken, causes changes. The Holy Spirit makes the Word of God which is real in the spirit realm, real to a person, even a physical reality; He makes it happen; He brings it to pass. This is how Jesus came to be.

"And the <u>Word became flesh</u> and dwelt among us…" - John 1:14

The Holy Spirit made the Word of God into a physical tangible reality in human form. This person was named Jesus of Nazareth (Luke 1:30-35). The Holy Spirit has the duty of making the Word of God real to the unbeliever that they may become a believer. This is how faith for salvation is imparted.

"[8] For by grace you have been <u>saved through faith</u>, and that not of yourselves; it is <u>the gift of God</u>, [9] not of works, lest anyone should boast. - Ephesians 2:8-9

This means that it is God who gives both the grace and faith needed for salvation that comes from continuous hearing of God's Word *(Romans 10:17; Ephesians 4:19)*. This is how a person is saved and becomes born-again because of the Gospel, but it is also the way we receive anything God has given to us in the Kingdom of God.

Once this occurs, the Word becomes manifest in the physical realm, as a confirmation that you have believed the Word of God to be true. Glory to God!

The Lord confirmed His Word in Revelation 21:4 some days after when I was watching a Gospel Channel. A Pastor and his wife were talking about how they dealt with the loss of their first daughter. They spoke about how the manner in which they comforted and ministered to the bereaving was enhanced ever since then, because they could now empathise with them. The pastor also mentioned that same Bible verse- *Revelation 21:4*. He said that God said that I should tell you that "there shall be no more death". I had no doubt in my heart that God was speaking to me. I would have many other experiences like this; where the Lord would bring His Word to me.

In every season we should be calm to hear from God because He has a Word for us. Get rid of the noise of society, the media, and the size of our problem. Rather look to the Word of God, and see how big our God is!

Know that just because the Holy Spirit brings the Word of God to us is not an excuse to not pick up the Bible and open it by oneself. The Holy Spirit has already brought the Word of God to the world when He conducted the writing and the collation of the Bible *(2 Peter 1:20-21)*. Although, He still brings the Word of God to us and directs us to what part of His Word we are to focus on per season.

II
The Ministry of the Holy Spirit in bringing Comfort, Strength, and Edification:

The Word of God ministered to the believer by the Holy Spirit is enough to bring about comfort *(Romans 15:4)*, strength *(Psalm 73:26)*, and edification *(1 Corinthian 14:3)*. However, the Lord by His Spirit has allowed it to be so that in our Christian walk, we experience various consolations of our faith that build us up, and incentives that motivates and encourages us. Every step of the way, even now I see Him constantly do this. Another medium through which He brings comfort is through people. There were several instances that He would send people my way. My interactions with them brought me strength, edification, and hope.

On our way back to Dublin, after meeting Pastor E.A. Adeboye, we met a certain woman at the departure gate in the airport, whose story inspired me. She noticed Prosper's condition and how I was attending to him. Being moved by it, she came and enquired of what had happened to Prosper. And I had nothing to hide. I explained everything as it was. She too opened up to me. She told me of how after being married for seven years, she gave birth to her daughter who had Down syndrome. And although her daughter had started to learn how to speak at four years of age, she remained thankful to God that she had a child who could call her "mummy". Her story touched my heart and made me appreciate God more. What He had done for me already could not be compared to what was presently happening. It was as if my Spirit rose to a new level of edification in that moment. Was the Holy Spirit preparing my heart for the incident that was about to happen on the plane?

Another time of strengthening was when Prosper died on the plane. There was a man of God on-board who God used to comfort me. Till this day, I thank God for his presence on the plane. I thought that I needed to be left alone. But on the contrary what I needed was help. It was meant to be Prosper and I coming home, but I was all on my own. The man of God spoke God's Word into my life and it comforted me. His voice was so calming, I felt relieved like I was given painkillers to soothe my soul. He held my hand throughout the remainder of the journey. His presence felt like Isaiah 43:2-4 in experience:

"When you go through deep waters, I will be with you. When you go through rivers of difficulty, you will not drown. When you walk through the fire of oppression, you will not be burned up; the flames will not consume you..." *Isaiah 43:2-4 (NLT)*

Moments like these where the Lord brought me comfort, edification, and strength were key moments to my healing journey.

III

The Ministry of the Holy Spirit in Manipulating my Desires and Emotions:

The Bible says that we are to "work out our salvation" in *Philippians 2:12,* Apostle Paul's (the writer of the epistle) reason for this is that "for it is God who works in us both to do and will His good pleasure" (*Philippians 2:13).* Working out our salvation is living out the salvation that God has given us and the benefits of it to produce much fruit in our lives through faith. One of the benefits of salvation is that the Holy Spirit is permitted to work on our will, desires, and emotions *(Philippians 2:13).* When healing from the loss of my son, this part of His ministry was profound. I found that I was receiving my healing gradually the more I spent time with Him. I constantly surrounded myself with His Word, edifying Gospel music, and immersed myself in church activities. This all contributed to my healing and growth a lot. For example, for the first two years or so since Prosper's death, I found it difficult to say his name or talk about him without feeling a heavy weight of sorrow in my chest and tears rolling down my cheeks. However, now I love talking about my son and I even have an event planning decor & catering business named after him. Glory to God!

I am more focused on God now than ever before. My desire for God and things of God has escalated. I enjoy spending my time in the presence of the Lord.

The Holy Spirit has been and still is a key part of my healing process and my daily Christian walk. With His help, my mental health was restored, I started going out again and resumed my customary occupations, such as travelling with my children and husband again.

After a few months, I became pregnant. I gave birth to a bouncing baby girl. I named her Promise after the revelation of God's promise to me in *(Revelations 21:4)*. Hallelujah, our God is faithful! Anytime I open my mouth to speak about the promise that God gave me, I feel peace in my heart.

Now the memory of Prosper abides with us; my family and I. I am now able to talk about him, the times that we spent together, and mention his beautiful name, happily. I love to call his name. I can now pray the prayer that used to make me cry, joyfully: *"whatever you lay your hands on will prosper"*. And so shall it be for you in Jesus name!

Part 2
The Edifying Word of God

"Now I commit you to God and to the word of his grace, which can build [edify] you up and give you an inheritance among all those who are sanctified. - Acts 20:32

"For the Word of God is quick [living] and powerful, and sharper than any twoedged sword, piercing even to the dividing asunder [division] of soul and spirit, and of the joints and marrow, and is a discerner of the thoughts and intents of the heart." - Hebrews 4:12 (KJV)

It goes without saying that the Word of God has played a significant role throughout the course of history, and in many generations, even before our time. The Word of God created the world *(John 1:3)*. God's Word prophesied the greatest event in history- the Messiah, throughout the Old Testament (with a few examples of *Daniel 9:25, Isaiah 7:24, Psalm 22)*, and even the future end to come as seen in the Book of Revelation. The Word of God is not just limited to the Bible that we have on our shelves or phones. It is the infinite knowledge of God; everything that God knows and everything about Him. Although, the Bible is the standard used to judge, if any other word outside of the Bible is truly the Word of God. The Word of God can take up many forms, including written form (e.g. the Bible), a spoken form (e.g. words of knowledge), and even human form (Jesus Christ our Lord). However, no matter what form the Word takes, the Word of God is a living entity and personality because God has breathed His eternal life into His Word.

"God has transmitted his very substance into every Scripture, for it is God-breathed…" - 2 Timothy 3:16 (TPT)

You can speak with the Word and the Word can speak to you as it is alive.

"When thou goest, it shall lead thee; when thou sleepest, it shall keep thee; and when thou awakest, it shall talk with thee." - Proverbs 6:22 (KJV)

The Function of the Word, among many, is to:

1.   Give Life and bring to life.

"For they are life to those who find them, And health to all their flesh." - Proverbs 4:22

2.   Shape & create realities

"All things were made through Him, and without Him nothing was made that was made." - John 1:3

3.   Reveal, Illuminate, and Enlighten

"[105] Thy word is a lamp unto my feet, and a light unto my path. [130] The entrance of thy words giveth light; it giveth understanding unto the simple." - Psalm 119:105, 13

4.   Protect

"And take the helmet of salvation, and the sword of the Spirit, which is the word of God;" - Ephesians 6:17

5.   Strengthen & Equip

"[16] All Scripture…is profitable for doctrine, for reproof, for correction, for instruction in righteousness, [17] that the man of God may be complete, thoroughly equipped for every good work." - 2 Timothy 3:16-17

The Word of God is not limited by the laws of the universe because the Word existed before the universe. It can therefore time-travel, and penetrate places that human hands cannot reach, e.g. the soul and spirit of man (Hebrews 4:12-13). Therefore, it was able to play a major role in my speedy edification, recovery, and restoration from the wound, bruises, and hurt of my son's death. Here are some examples of words of edification and comfort contained in this Word of God:

"Finally, brethren, whatever things are true, whatever things are noble, whatever things are just, whatever things are pure, whatever things are lovely, whatever things are of good report, if there is any virtue and if there is anything praiseworthy—meditate on these things" - Philippians 4:8

"A time to weep, And a time to laugh; A time to mourn, And a time to dance;" - Ecclesiastes 3:4

"And God will wipe away every tear from their eyes; there shall be no more death, nor sorrow, nor crying. There shall be no more pain, for the former things have passed away." - Revelation 21:4

"[5] Trust in the Lord with all your heart, And lean not on your own understanding; [6] In all your ways acknowledge Him, And He shall direct your paths." - Proverbs 3:5-6

CHAPTER FOUR

Memories & Tributes

"For I consider that the sufferings of this present time are not worthy to be compared with the glory which shall be revealed in us." - Romans 8:18

"Therefore you now have sorrow; but I will see you again and your heart will rejoice, and your joy no one will take from you." - John 16:22

This chapter contains tributes and poems of Prosper, showing how in grief, one can find grace. Grief can open one's eye to see a lot of things in our lives and in the world, including discovering the grace of God.

My Letter to My Younger Brother

28th February 2019

Dear Prosper,

How's it been? It's been a while since we last talked
I remember our last conversation;
Our last discussion;
Our last consociation.
Unfortunately, it was over the telephone.
But if I had known that you would leave so soon, I would have been in
your presence, yeah, present with you.

On Saturday the 21st of May, you were born to two,
Who never knew that they would mourn
When they would see you no more.
It was in that labour room in the Coombe
That they cuddled, huddled, and hugged you
So tightly, like they knew they were going to lose you.

And ever since you gone, I've found myself constantly asking:
"Is it better to be three years younger-dead, or three years older-alive?"
To be or not to be, that is the question;
that is the contemplation;
that is the comparison

Either way your body would still decay,
as your dead cells harden and fall to the ground,

comes new skin buried underground;
underneath the old,
Comes out the new
Comes out the new
Comes out the new

I never thought that we would encounter death,
I never expected it to befall our family
But without an invitation, he came uninvited
Like an unwanted guest at a party,
He welcomed himself to the family
Unlike other burglars who would break-in sneakily,
Going after material things to steal cunningly
No! This burglar was like no other
He did not come and go, he came to stay

Although, the progression of his stay was slow
Short, small, slim,
He walked in unexpectedly,
Then stood still happily,
And finally, sat down on our couch, comfortably
Making our home, his home,
Our family, his family,
Our family, his family
Our family, his family

 Wanting to increase his comfortability, but there was no room for him
to stretch his legs
And seeing that he sat down next to you,
His only option was to get rid of you.

We offered him our peace, our dignity, and our privacy,
But he refused to receive them, he had your life in mind hungrily
But he was not swift to eat you up like meat,
He took hold of your body, but only increased his grip slowly
Like Bridget's blanket, his legs stretched steadily,
Like bacteria, his territory grew exponentially,
Oh, did he kill you softly,
Oh, did he kill you softly,
Oh, did he kill you softly

He was a bug to your belly,
The darkness (the colour of death) that filled the pupils of your eyes and took away your eyesight
And as he increased his grip, you lost yours,
He seized your body when he paralysed it with a seizure.

 I couldn't see it,
I wouldn't believe it,
because I refused to acknowledge it,
until our mother confirmed it
He forced our eyes to behold him eat you up,
With his fork of sickness & his knife of illness,
You were served on a plate of darkness
And all we could do was to watch & pray hopefully

I admire your strength,
For you refused to bow to death,
An aggressive warrior who fought even 'til his death

Yet God is merciful, faithful, dependable,
Perfecting your passing away,

When on the Sunday, the seventh day,
You died and ascended in the sky

Seventeen months death lingered in our family,
But on the seventh month came,
A baby girl named,
With the Promise that God said to our family:

"And I shall wipe away the tears from thine eyes,
And there shall be no more death,
Neither sorrow, nor crying,
Neither shall there be any more pain,
For the former things have passed away"
Truly your death was that dark night we awaited the dawning of a new
day...

"It's been a long day without you my friend,
And I'll tell you all about it when I see you again,
We've come a long way from where we began,
And I'll tell you all about it when I see you again,
When I see you again..."

Yours Sincerely,
Your Sista,
Peace Onakoya.

P.S. Now we share the month of February,
      My birthday, and your anniversary.

Peace Onakoya

Letter from Manchester United Footbal Club

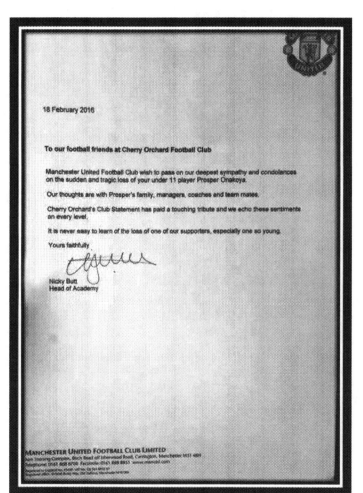

18 February 2016

To our football friends at Cherry Orchard Football Club

Manchester United Football Club wish to pass on our deepest sympathy and condolences on the sudden and tragic loss of your under 11 player Prosper Onakoya.

Our thoughts are with Prosper's family, managers, coaches and team mates.

Cherry Orchard's Club Statement has paid a touching tribute and we echo these sentiments on every level.

It is never easy to learn of the loss of one of our supporters, especially one so young.

Yours faithfully

Nicky Butt
Head of Academy

MANCHESTER UNITED FOOTBALL CLUB LIMITED
Aon Training Complex, Birch Road off Isherwood Road, Carrington, Manchester M31 4BH
Telephone: 0161 868 8700 Facsimile: 0161 868 8855 www.manutd.com

CHAPTER FIVE
Receiving Jesus & His Holy Spirit

"[28] Come to Me, all you who labour and are heavy laden, and I will give you rest. [29] Take My yoke upon you and learn from Me, for I am gentle and lowly in heart, and you will find rest for your souls." Jesus Christ (Matthew 11:28-29)

I

Receiving Jesus:

The grace of God is a gift of God that He has freely given to all of mankind out of His love for them. The grace of God unfailingly brings ease to the life of everyone who is in possession of it. It attracts into the life of the possessor effortlessly any and every thing good. It turns deserts into rivers, barrenness to fruitfulness, sorrow to joy, despair to hope, weakness to strength, bondage to salvation, and darkness to light. The grace of God eliminates struggle and hardship, and it is definitely something a person should not reject, especially since it has been made a free gift to all mankind. You would have to hate yourself to ignore the grace of God.

"[14] And the Word became flesh and dwelt among us,…full of grace and truth. [17] For the law was given through Moses, but grace and truth came through Jesus Christ. - John 1:14, 17

This grace of God is encapsulated in the person of Jesus Christ Himself.

Just like in medication, the actual substance is in the capsule, but you have to accept the capsule in order to receive the substance. Even so, to receive this grace of God, you must accept Jesus into your life. He is not only the capsule containing the grace of God, He is the very grace of God Himself. When you have received Jesus, you receive the grace of God. Who is this Jesus I introduce to you? He is the very God in the flesh *(John 1:1, 14)*; the Son of God who brings salvation to all men *(Titus 2:11)*, to as many as will accept Him, making them children of God *(John 1:12-13)*. This is the revelation of who Jesus is and what He came to do, thus His name means salvation *(Matthew 1:21)*. Therefore, the grace of God is received when a person accepts the salvation of God, and vice versa *(Ephesians 2:8)*. God tells us in the Bible that the way we receive this salvation is through believing in the Lord Jesus (who He is, that He died for our sins and resurrected, and its implications) and confessing His Lordship over our life.

"[9] that if you <u>confess with your mouth the Lord Jesus and believe in your heart that God has raised Him from the dead, you will be saved.</u> [10] For with the heart one believes unto righteousness, and with the mouth confession is made unto salvation." - Romans 10:9-10

You <u>cannot</u> become a Christian and go to Heaven by solely attending church service(s), by good deeds, or doing godly activities. You must believe in and accept the Lordship of Jesus; the salvation of God over your life, and say that you do so. It is a matter of life and death *(Proverbs 18:21; Matthew 12:37)* and only you can receive Jesus for you, no one else can. Only then would your godly activities have meaning. And if you do so, saying the following confession, God says that you become a completely new person *(2 Corinthians 5:17)*, born of God *(John 1:12-13)*, who is righteous (Romans 3:22-26), and has God's eternal life (John 3:16).

Confession:

"Lord God, I believe with all my heart in Jesus Christ, the Son of the living God. I believe that He died for me and God raised Him from the dead. I believe He's alive today. I confess with my mouth that Jesus Christ is Lord of my life from this day and forever. Through Him and in His name, I have eternal life; I am born again. I have the grace of God and I am saved. Thank you Lord for this gift! I am now a child of God. Hallelujah!"

Congratulations! You are now born of Almighty God!

II

The Baptism with the Holy Spirit:

Before Jesus died and resurrected, He said He had to return to the Father in Heaven in order for the Holy Spirit to be given.

"[5] But now I go away to Him who sent Me [God the Father], and none of you asks Me, 'Where are You going?' [7] Nevertheless I tell you the truth. It is to your advantage that I go away; for if I do not go away, the Helper will not come to you; but if I depart, I will send Him to you." - John 16:5, 7

The presence of the Holy Spirit in earth is the proof that Jesus truly has ascended to the Father. Jesus calls Him in this verse 'the Helper', in the original rendering this name means intercessor; consoler; advocate; comforter. Jesus says that having this Holy Spirit is to our advantage. Having Him gives one the edge in life.

Now that you are born again, it is expedient that you receive this Holy Spirit as He is the key to actually living and experiencing this glorious, triumphant, and victorious life that you have received. Without a relationship with Him, we will live defeated as if we were not actually born of God.

The Holy Spirit does not force Himself on anyone, even though He wholeheartedly wants to help you. Nonetheless, if you would genuinely ask for the Holy Spirit, God the Father will most definitely with no exception give Him to you freely.

"If you then, being evil, know how to give good gifts to your children, how much more will your heavenly Father give the Holy Spirit to those who ask Him!" Luke 11:13

The Holy Spirit is the gift of God to His children that God lavishes upon them, fulfilling the His Word spoken through the Prophet Joel in *Joel 2:28.*

Every time the Holy Spirit has been received, He brings God's language which He gives the Christian power to speak. This is known as speaking/praying with the Spirit, or in tongues. This language is a supernatural language with supernatural capabilities and abilities that are dynamic in their working to cause miraculous changes without fail. We see the effects of the baptism with the Holy Spirit and His divine language in the early church (Acts 2) and even now.

If you would like to receive the Holy Spirit, ask for Him saying the following prayer. You must believe that you have received Him once you do so because God said that is what will happen unfailingly:

Prayer:

"Heavenly Father, I realise and acknowledge that I need your Holy Spirit to live the triumphant life you have called me to live. So today I ask for Him in Jesus name. I receive the Holy Spirit upon me right now. Holy Spirit, I welcome you into my life. I am your portal into the physical world. Thank you for remaining with me from now and for eternity."

The divine language of God the Holy Spirit will begin to bubble up from the inside of you as syllables that the human mind cannot naturally comprehend and finds strange (Acts 2:4). Do not doubt it, it is a real language that God understands as you speak it (1 Corinthians 14:2). As you speak the language out in faith, you are releasing the power of God that edifies you (1 Corinthians 14:4; Jude 20). You can speak this language at will whenever you like. It is yours to speak expressly now!

If you have made one or more of these greatest decisions to receive the Lord Jesus Christ and/or His Holy Spirit, please let us know and contact us: infogoandprosperservices@gmail.com.

About Go and Prosper

Printed in the United States
by Baker & Taylor Publisher Services